To: _____

From: _____

Date: _____

*Because there is one loaf, we, who are many,*
*are one body, for we all share the one loaf.*

—1 Corinthians 10:17


For Christie and Tyler. Two of my favorites to receive communion from.
—Glenys


For my mom. I love you mommy.
—Anna Kazimi

ZONDERKIDZ

*Gathered at the Table*
Copyright © 2024 by Glenys Nellist
Illustration © 2024 by Glenys Nellist

Requests for information should be addressed to:
customercare@harpercollins.com

Published in Grand Rapids, Michigan, by Zonderkidz. Zonderkidz is a registered trademark of The Zondervan Corporation, L.L.C., a wholly owned subsidiary of HarperCollins Christian Publishing, Inc.

Hardcover: ISBN 978-0-310-15536-2
Ebook: ISBN 978-0-310-15560-7

*Illustrations: Anna Kazimi*
*Editor: Megan Dobson*
*Art direction and design: Cindy Davis*

*Printed in Malaysia*

24 25 26 27 28 /IMG/ 20 19 18 17 16 15 14 13 12 11 10 9 8 7 6 5 4 3 2 1

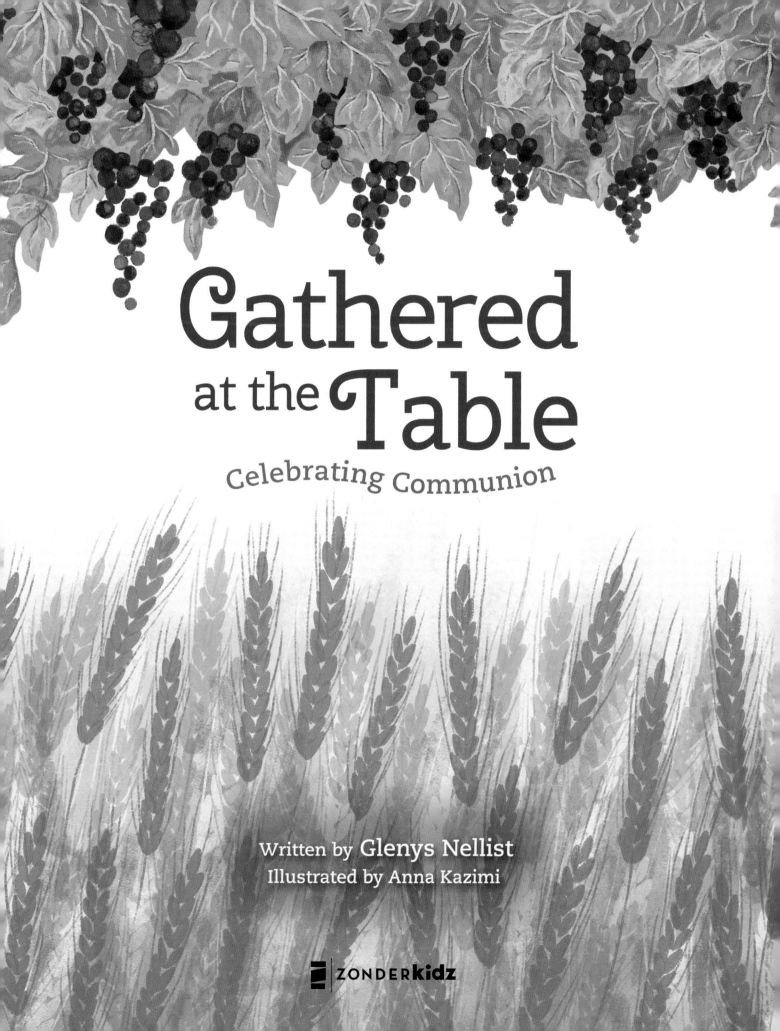

# Gathered
## at the Table
### Celebrating Communion

Written by **Glenys Nellist**
Illustrated by Anna Kazimi

ZONDER**kidz**

Communion is a beautiful, holy, mysterious gift. When we gather at the table to share bread and wine, God's invisible Spirit hovers in the air, just like it did over two thousand years ago, when Jesus gathered with his disciples in the upper room ...

It was evening in Jerusalem. Jesus knew he didn't have long to live on Earth. What could he do to help his friends remember how he had lived and loved?

Jesus did something very special. In the quietness of that room, Jesus called his disciples to the table. As they watched and listened, Jesus took bread, gave thanks, broke it, and gave it to each of them. Then he took wine, poured it out, and gave that to his disciples too. And as he did, Jesus softly said, "Whenever you eat bread, remember me. Whenever you drink wine, remember me."

Called to the table,
To share the wine and bread.
"I want you to remember me,"
Jesus softly said.

Ever since that night, Christians all around the world are called to the table too, as we celebrate communion and remember Jesus. We hear the mysterious words Jesus spoke to his disciples …

"This is my body. It is given for you. Every time you eat it, do this in memory of me. This cup is the new covenant in my blood. It is poured out for you." And we wonder what those mysterious words might mean for us ...

We think about the mystery—
The words that Jesus said,
And how he gave his life for us
As we break the bread.

There are different names for this special meal. It can be called *Holy Communion*, *the Lord's Supper*, or *the Eucharist*. The bread can be one large loaf or little wafers. The wine or grape juice can be in one large cup or little ones.

We may gather around a table, kneel at an altar, or stay in our seats. But no matter what this special meal is called, and no matter how we receive it, we remember as we take communion that Jesus chose to give his life for us. What wonderful love!

Gathered at the table,
God's Spirit in the air,
We drink the cup of blessing,
The bread of life we share.

Some children attend a special class to learn all about communion and what it means. Their First Holy Communion is a very special, exciting event and all the family celebrates. In other churches, even babies are welcome to take communion!

But no matter how old we are, whether we attend a class or not, we know that in communion, we are one family, joined together in the love of Jesus.

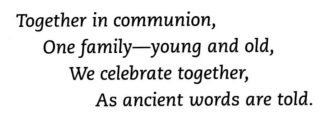

Together in communion,
One family—young and old,
We celebrate together,
As ancient words are told.

When we get ready to take communion, Jesus knows exactly how we feel. If our hearts are heavy or sad, if we've messed up or feel unloved, Jesus knows. And as we reach out for the bread and wine, Jesus reaches out to us and fills us with love, forgiveness, and hope.

There's room at the table,
No matter how we feel.
Jesus reaches out to us
In this holy meal.

As we leave the communion table, God's presence goes with us. We step out into the world, reminded of how Jesus taught us to live and love. We rise from the table wrapped in the goodness and grace of God—forgiven, loved, and called to share the love of Jesus however and wherever we can.

We rise from the table,
Forgiven, loved, and free.
We leave to be the people
Who God calls us to be.

One special day every year, millions of Christians all around the world celebrate World Communion Sunday. Indoors and outdoors, in churches and homes, in cities and on farms, by lakeshores and under tents, people remember Jesus as they break bread.

The bread might be brown or white; large or little; flat or fluffy. But the color and size and kind don't matter. What matters is that just like the different breads, each one of us represents one big, beautiful, diversely different family, gathered across God's globe, to remember Jesus.

Gathered at the table,
Surrounded by God's grace,
We are one Christian family
In every time and place.

No matter *how* or *where* or *when* communion is celebrated, Jesus stands at the head of every table, reaches out his hands, smiles, and says,

## Come. Come to the table.

People will come from east and west and north and south.
They will take their places at the feast in God's kingdom.

Luke 13:29 (NIrV)